THAILAND

Written by Sadie Hallworth

COUNTRIES of the WORLD

PowerKiDS press

Published in 2025
by The Rosen Publishing Group, Inc.
2544 Clinton Street, Buffalo, NY 14224

Written by: Sadie Hallworth
Edited by: Elise Carraway
Designed by: Ker Ker Lee

Cataloging-in-Publication Data

Names: Hallworth, Sadie.
Title: Thailand / Sadie Hallworth.
Description: Buffalo, NY : PowerKids Press, 2025. | Series: Countries of the world | Includes glossary and index.
Identifiers: ISBN 9781499447309 (pbk.) | ISBN 9781499447316 (library bound) | ISBN 9781499447323 (ebook)
Subjects: LCSH: Thailand--Juvenile literature.
Classification: LCC DS563.5 H355 2025 | DDC 959.3--dc23

Manufactured in the United States of America
CPSIA Compliance Information: Batch #CSPK25. For further information contact Rosen Publishing at 1-800-237-9932.

Find us on

Image Credits
All images are courtesy of Shutterstock.com, unless otherwise specified. With thanks to Getty Images, Thinkstock Photo and iStockphoto. Cover – AlexAnton, OAnderson, aphotostory, Kidsada Manchinda, saravutpics. 2 – Travel mania. 4–5 – Andrei Minsk, Travel mania. 6–7 – BAMBELL, Pichet suriya. 8–9 – HacKLeR, Sakdawut Tangtongsap. 10–11 –annop26, Nattakorn_Maneerat. 12–13 – POP-THAILAND, AlivePhoto. 14–15 –Travel mania, Torychemistry. 16–17 – Raksan36studio, APChanel. 18–19 – photofriday, 1000 Words. 20–21 – Golf Photographer, bluedog studio. 22–23 – Ninja SS, siriwat sriphojaroen.

CONTENTS

Words that look like this can be found in the glossary on page 24.

WHERE IS THAILAND?

Thailand is a country found in Southeast Asia. It is surrounded by Myanmar, Laos, Cambodia, Malaysia, and the Gulf of Thailand.

The capital city of Thailand is Bangkok. Thailand's official language is Thai.

LANDSCAPE AND WEATHER

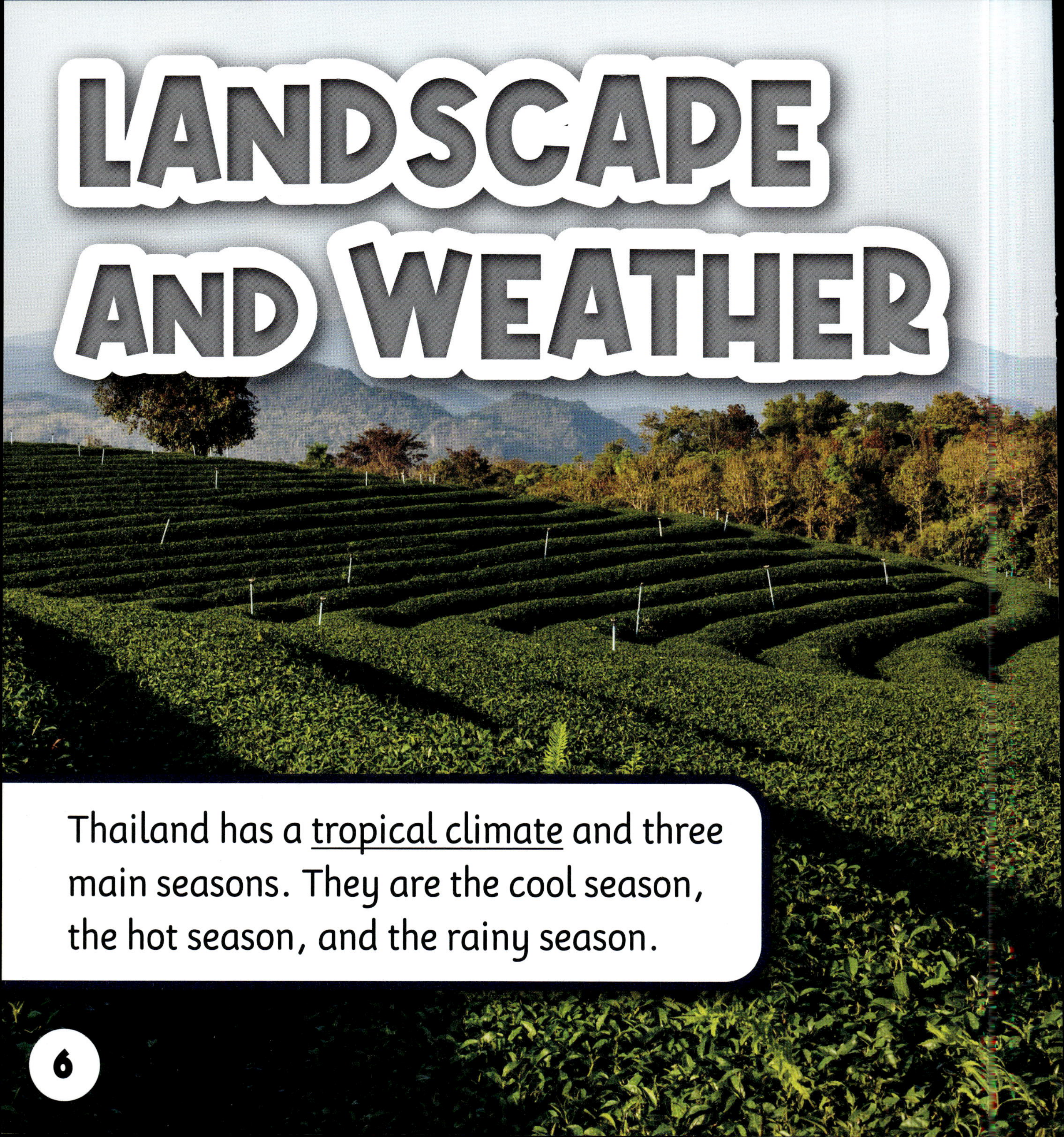

Thailand has a tropical climate and three main seasons. They are the cool season, the hot season, and the rainy season.

Thailand has many different landscapes. It has sandy beaches, mountains, flowing rivers, and over 1,400 islands.

Doi Inthanon has the highest mountain peak in Thailand at 8,415 feet (2,565 m) above sea level.

Doi Inthanon National Park, Thailand

RELIGION

The religion with the most followers in Thailand is Buddhism. There are over 40,000 temples in Thailand. Temples are where Buddhists worship.

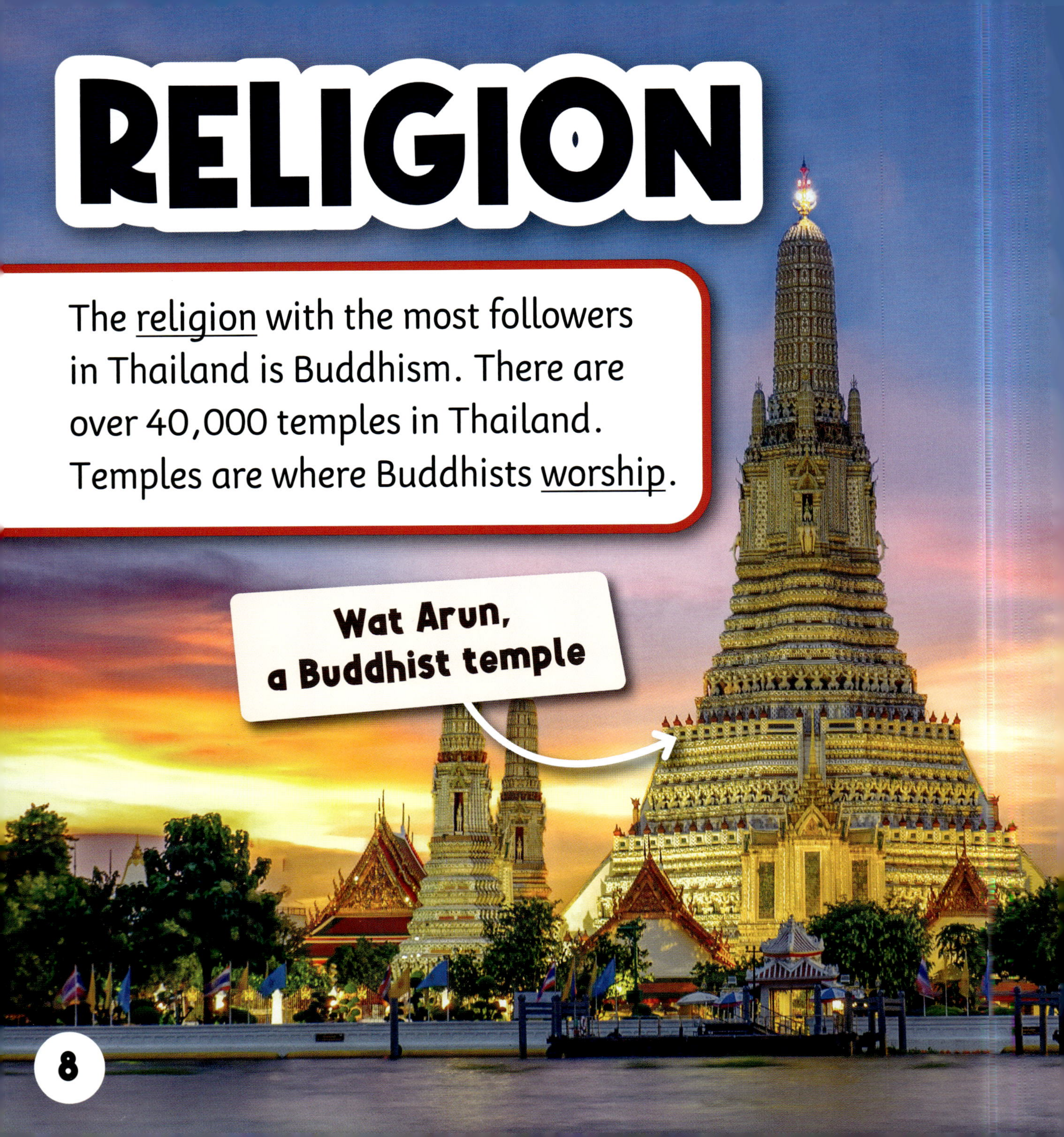

Wat Arun, a Buddhist temple

Some Buddhists, called monks, follow a strict set of rules that help them to live a simple and kind life. They often wear traditional orange robes.

These orange robes are called Kasaya.

FAMILIES

Many children in Thailand live with their parents and brothers and sisters at home. They may also live with other family members, such as their grandparents.

Thai families like to get together to celebrate special occasions such as religious festivals. They often celebrate by eating special food and singing songs.

SCHOOL

Children in Thailand go to school from the age of 6 and usually finish when they are 18. They study Thai, math, science, and religion.

Thai children also study a foreign language. They can study languages such as Chinese, French, Japanese, Russian, German, or English.

HOME

Many families live in small villages. Lots of people who live in villages work on farms growing crops, such as rice.

Many people in Thailand live in big cities. They often live and work in tall, modern buildings.

CLOTHING

Many people in Thailand wear modern clothing. There are also many parts of Thailand where traditional clothing is still worn, especially for special events.

Traditional Thai clothing is usually very bright and colorful. Women often wear long dresses made from embroidered silk.

SPORTS

Muay Thai is a type of boxing that is very popular in Thailand. Two people fight each other by using their knees, shins, elbows, and fists. It takes a lot of skill and practice.

Other popular sports in Thailand include volleyball, basketball, and soccer. Many children learn how to swim and play sports at school.

FOOD

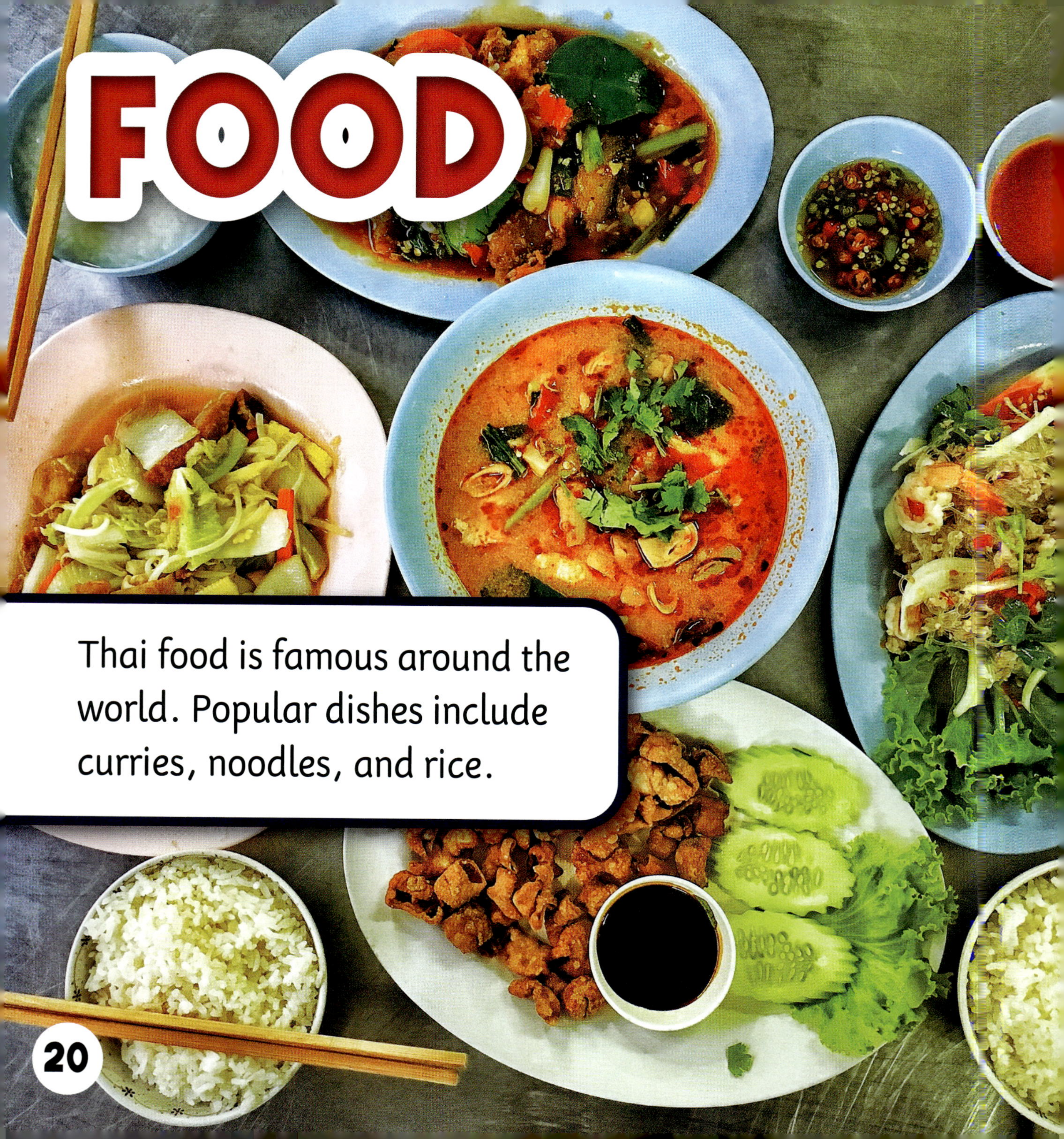

Thai food is famous around the world. Popular dishes include curries, noodles, and rice.

Rice dishes are eaten using a spoon and a fork. Even noodle dishes are often eaten with a spoon and fork, but chopsticks and a spoon may sometimes be used instead.

FUN FACTS

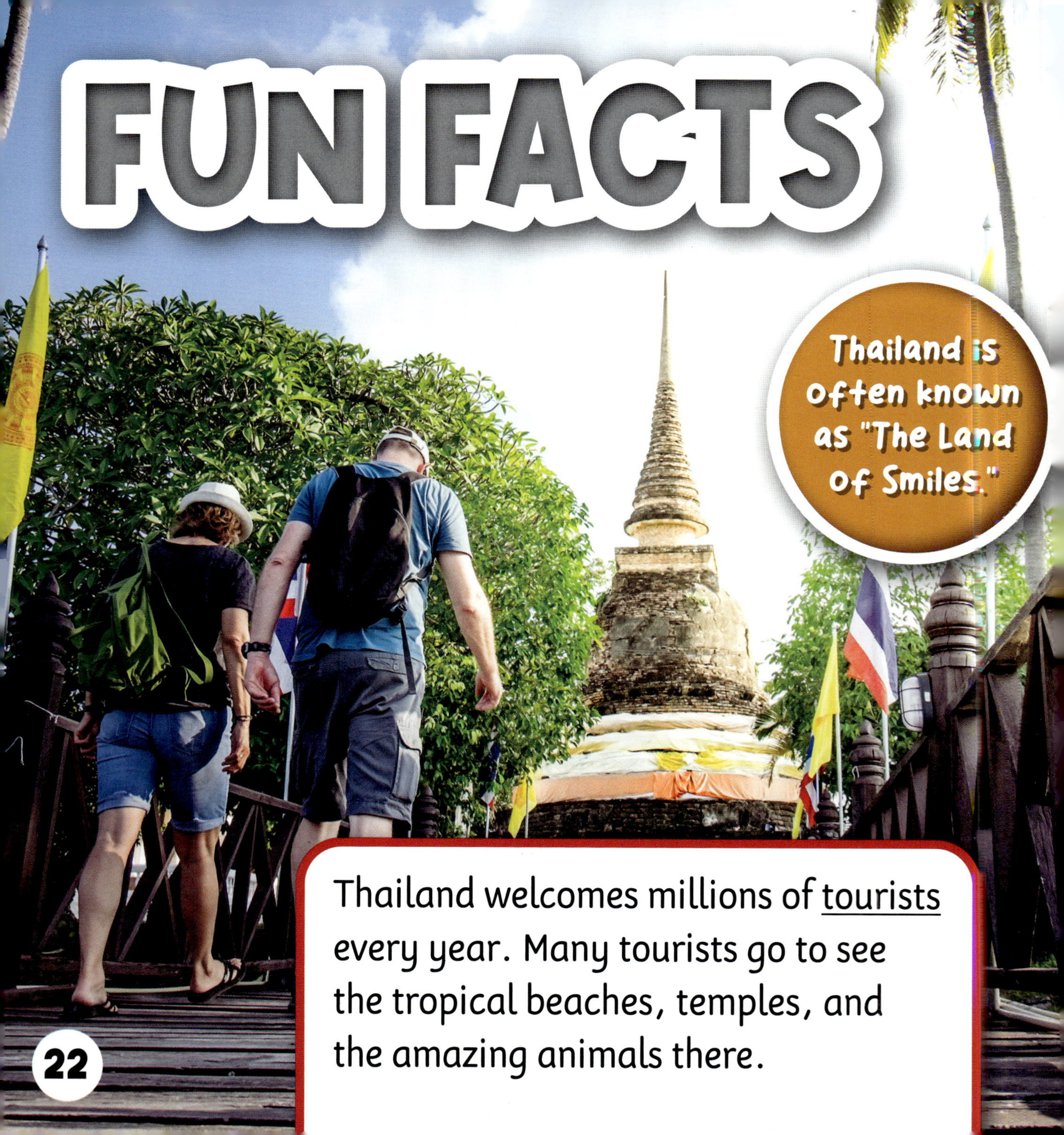

Thailand is often known as "The Land of Smiles."

Thailand welcomes millions of <u>tourists</u> every year. Many tourists go to see the tropical beaches, temples, and the amazing animals there.

Traditional Thai stories are full of interesting creatures such as ghosts and magical animals. There are hundreds of fairy tales that are still told to children today.

GLOSSARY

embroidered having patterns sewn into fabric

festivals times when people come together to celebrate special events

foreign to do with another country or language

modern to do with recent or present times

official to do with something that is recognized as having power or being important

religion a system of faith and worship, especially to do with a god or gods

tourists people who visit another place for pleasure

traditional to do with beliefs, customs, or ways of behaving that have been around for a long time

tropical climate warm and wet weather

worship religious acts of praise, such as prayer

INDEX